W9-AHA-596

KEY FIGURES OF
THE KOREAN WAR

BIOGRAPHIES OF WAR

KEY FIGURES OF

THE KOREAN WAR

EDITED BY
SHAUN SETH

Britannica®
Educational Publishing

IN ASSOCIATION WITH

ROSEN
EDUCATIONAL SERVICES

Published in 2016 by Britannica Educational Publishing (a trademark of Encyclopædia Britannica, Inc.) in association with The Rosen Publishing Group, Inc.
29 East 21st Street, New York, NY 10010

Distributed exclusively by Rosen Publishing.
To see additional Britannica Educational Publishing titles, go to rosenpublishing.com.

First Edition

Britannica Educational Publishing
J. E. Luebering: Director, Core Reference Group
Anthony L. Green: Editor, Compton's by Britannica

Rosen Publishing
Hope Lourie Killcoyne: Executive Editor
Nelson Sá: Art Director
Shaun Seth: Editor
Michael Moy: Designer
Cindy Reiman: Photography Manager

Library of Congress Cataloging-in-Publication Data

Key figures of the Korean War/edited by Shaun Seth.—First edition.
    pages cm.—(Biographies of war)
Includes bibliographical references and index.
Audience: Grades 7–12.
ISBN 978-1-68048-060-3 (library bound)
1. Korean War, 1950–1953—Biography—Juvenile literature. I. Seth, Shaun.
DS918.A553K49 2015
 951.904'20922—dc23
                                                                                2014045465

Manufactured in the United States of America

On the cover: (Foreground) Former U.S. President Harry Truman (left) shakes hands with South Korean president Syngman Rhee, c. 1954, not long after the end of the Korean War. (Background) U.S. troops exit tandem helicopters in a field during the Korean War.

CONTENTS

The roots of the Korean War are deeply embedded in history. While few regions are less suited to warfare than is the mountainous, river-slashed Korean peninsula, few have known more conflict. For centuries, Korea's three powerful neighbors—China, Japan, and Russia—vied for its control. By 1910, Japan had established a supremacy that it was to maintain until its defeat in World War II.

Seven days before the Japanese surrender that ended World War II, the Soviet Union (officially established in 1922) declared war on Japan. Soviet troops entered Korea. By agreement, the Soviet Union accepted the surrender of all Japanese forces in Korea north of the 38th parallel of latitude, while the United States accepted the surrender of Japanese units south of the 38th parallel.

The Soviet Union quickly sealed off the 38th-parallel border. It soon set up an interim civil government for the nine million Koreans of the north, which contained most of Korea's industry. The government was run by Soviet-trained Communist officials.

The Korean War Veterans Memorial in Washington, D.C., honors American men and women who served in the Korean War.

The United States maintained a military government in the south. The 21 million Koreans of the largely agricultural region were not satisfied with it.

A United States–Soviet commission that was established to make plans for the reunification of Korea under a free government made no progress. In 1947 the United States took the problem before the United Nations, which voted that free elections—under its supervision—should be held throughout Korea in 1948 to choose a single government. The Soviet Union refused to permit the United Nations election commission to enter the north. Elections were thus held only in the south, where a National Assembly and a president—Syngman Rhee—were chosen. The new democracy was named the Republic of Korea (South Korea).

In the north, the Soviet Union proclaimed a Communist dictatorship called the Democratic People's Republic of Korea (North Korea). P'yŏngyang was named its capital. Late in 1948, Soviet forces began to withdraw from North Korea, leaving behind an entrenched Communist regime and a well-trained, well-equipped North Korean army. United States occupation forces left South Korea in 1949. They left behind a government still "feeling its way" and an army ill-trained compared with that of the north. This army also lacked air power, tanks, and artillery.

South Korea, however, successfully resisted North Korean attempts at subversion, Communist-supported guerrilla activities, and border raids by North Korean forces. Frustrated, North Korea early in

1950 decided upon war to achieve its goal of Korean unification under Communist rule.

In June 1950 North Korea's army totaled 135,000 men. North Korea's infantry was also supported by approximately 150 Soviet-made medium tanks, ample artillery, and a small air force. South Korea's ground forces included a 45,000-member national police force and an army of 98,000. South Korea was armed largely with light infantry weapons supplied by the United States. It had no tanks or combat aircraft, and its artillery was inferior to that of North Korea. Its officers and enlisted men had generally less training and experience than did those of North Korea.

The United Nations, with the United States as the principal participant, joined the war on the side of the South Koreans, and the People's Republic of China came to North Korea's aid. At first North Korean troops drove the South Korean and U.S. forces down to the southern tip of the Korean peninsula, but a brilliant amphibious landing at Inch'ŏn, conceived by General Douglas MacArthur, turned the tide in favor of the UN troops, who advanced near the border of North Korea and China. The Chinese then entered the war and drove the UN forces back south; the front line stabilized at the 38th parallel.

After more than a million combat casualties had been suffered on both sides, the fighting ended in July 1953 with Korea still divided into two hostile states. Negotiations in 1954 produced no further agreement, and the front line has been accepted ever since as the de facto boundary between North and South Korea.

Although often referred to as the "Forgotten War," the conflict in Korea would have lasting effects on the world's geopolitical landscape and U.S. foreign policy for decades to come. Involving an international cast of figures at the height of the Cold War, the Korean War would also see remarkable political and military maneuvering as well as unforgettable sacrifice by those fighting for their countries and leaders. The events of the war and the stories of the individuals who fought on the front lines or in the political arena are surveyed in the following pages.

CHAPTER ONE

EARLY STAGES OF WAR

The Korean War had its immediate origins in the collapse of the Japanese empire at the end of World War II in September 1945. Unlike China, Manchuria, and the former Western colonies seized by Japan in 1941–42, Korea—annexed to Japan since 1910—did not have a native government or a colonial regime waiting to return after hostilities ceased. Most claimants to power were harried exiles in China, Manchuria, Japan, the U.S.S.R., and the United States. They fell into two broad categories. The first was made up of committed Marxist revolutionaries who had fought the Japanese as part of the Chinese-dominated guerrilla armies in Manchuria and China. One of these exiles was a minor but successful guerrilla leader named Kim Il-Sung, who had received some training in Russia and had been made a major in the Soviet army. The other Korean nationalist movement, no less revolutionary, drew its inspiration from the best of science, education, and industrialism in Europe, Japan, and

11

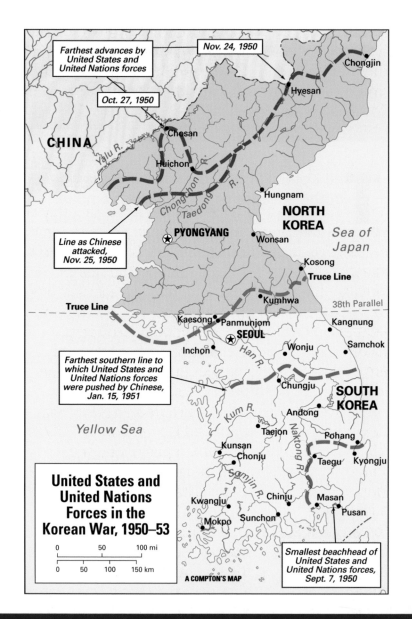

Farthest advances by
United States and
United Nations forces

Nov. 24, 1950

Chongjin

Oct. 27, 1950

Hyesan

CHINA

Chosan

Yalu R.

Huichon

Chongchon

Taedong R.

Hungnam

Line as Chinese
attacked,
Nov. 25, 1950

NORTH
KOREA

PYONGYANG

Wonsan

Sea of
Japan

Kosong

Truce Line

Truce Line

Kumhwa

38th Parallel

Kaesong • Panmunjom

Kangnung

SEOUL

Inchon

Han R.

Wonju

Samchok

Farthest southern line to
which United States and
United Nations forces
were pushed by Chinese,
Jan. 15, 1951

Chungju

SOUTH
KOREA

Kum R.

Andong

Yellow Sea

Taejon

Naktong R.

Pohang

Kunsan

Chonju

Taegu

Kyongju

Somjin R.

United States and
United Nations
Forces in the
Korean War, 1950–53

Kwangju

Chinju

Masan

Mokpo

Sunchon

Pusan

0		50		100 mi
0	50	100	150 km	

A COMPTON'S MAP

Smallest beachhead of
United States and
United Nations forces,
Sept. 7, 1950

This map shows how the conflict surged back and forth over the course
of the Korean War. The truce line added 850 square miles (2,200 square
kilometers) to North Korea below the 38th parallel; 2,350 square miles
(6,090 square kilometers) to South Korea above it.

America. These "ultranationalists" were split into rival factions, one of which centered on Syngman Rhee, educated in the United States and at one time the president of a dissident Korean Provisional Government in exile.

BUILDUP TO WAR

In their hurried effort to disarm the Japanese army and repatriate the Japanese population in Korea (estimated at 700,000), the United States and the Soviet Union agreed in August 1945 to divide the country for administrative purposes at the 38th parallel (latitude 38° N). At least from the American perspective, this geographic division was a temporary expedient; however, the Soviets began a short-lived reign of terror in northern Korea that quickly politicized the division by driving thousands of refugees south.

The two sides could not agree on a formula that would produce a unified Korea, and in 1947 U.S. President Harry S. Truman persuaded the United Nations (UN) to assume responsibility for the country, though the U.S. military remained nominally in control of the South until 1948. Both the South Korean national police and the constabulary doubled in size, providing a southern security force of about 80,000 by 1947. In the meantime, Kim Il-Sung strengthened his control over the Communist Party as well as the northern administrative structure and military forces. In 1948 the North Korean military and police numbered about 100,000, reinforced by

38TH PARALLEL

The 38th Parallel is the popular name given to latitude 38° N that in East Asia roughly demarcates North Korea and South Korea. The line was chosen by U.S. military planners at the Potsdam Conference (July 1945) near the end of World War II as an army boundary, north of which the U.S.S.R. was to accept the surrender of the Japanese forces in Korea and south of which the Americans were to accept the Japanese surrender. The line was intended as a temporary division of the country, but the onset of the Cold War led to the establishment of a separate U.S.-oriented regime in South Korea under Syngman Rhee and a Communist regime in North Korea under Kim Il-Sung.

After the outbreak of the Korean War between North and South Korea in June 1950, UN forces—which under U.S. General Douglas MacArthur had come to the aid of the South— moved north of the 38th parallel in an attempt to occupy North Korea. With the intervention of Chinese troops in support of the North, the war came to a stalemate roughly along that parallel. The cease-fire line, fixed at the time of the armistice agreement, gave South Korea possession of an eastern mountainous area north of the parallel, which was the major battlefront when the demarcation line was fixed. Likewise, North Korea was given a roughly triangular portion of territory south of the 38th parallel and west of longitude 127° E that includes the city of Kaesŏng.

U.S. president Harry S. Truman (*center*), Soviet premier Joseph Stalin (*left*), and British prime minister Winston Churchill (*right*) at the Potsdam Conference near Berlin, Germany, July 1945, where the decision to divide Korea at the 38th parallel was made.

a group of southern Korean guerrillas based at Haeju in western Korea.

The creation of an independent South Korea became UN policy in early 1948. Southern Communists opposed this, and by autumn partisan warfare had engulfed parts of every Korean province below the 38th parallel. The fighting expanded into a limited border war between the South's newly formed Republic of Korea Army (ROKA) and the North Korean border constabulary as well as the North's Korean People's Army (KPA). The North launched 10 cross-border guerrilla incursions in order to draw ROKA units away from their guerrilla-suppression campaign in the South.

In its larger purpose the partisan uprising failed: the Republic of Korea (ROK) was formed in August 1948, with Syngman Rhee as president. Nevertheless, almost 8,000 members of the South Korean security forces and at least 30,000 other Koreans lost their lives. Many of the victims were not security forces or armed guerrillas at all but simply people identified as "rightists" or "reds" by the belligerents. Small-scale atrocities became a way of life.

The partisan war also delayed the training of the South Korean army. In early 1950, American advisers judged that fewer than half of the ROKA's infantry battalions

were even marginally ready for war. U.S. military assistance consisted largely of surplus light weapons and supplies. Indeed, General Douglas MacArthur, commander of the United States' Far East Command (FECOM), argued that his Eighth Army, consisting of

General Douglas MacArthur (*right*) stands with South Korean president Syngman Rhee. After World War II, MacArthur oversaw the Allied occupation of Japan. He commanded UN forces after the outbreak of the Korean War.

four weak divisions in Japan, required more support than the Koreans.

In early 1949 Kim Il-Sung pressed his case with Soviet leader Joseph Stalin that the time had come for a conventional invasion of the South. Stalin refused, concerned about the relative unpreparedness of the North Korean armed forces and about possible U.S. involvement. In the course of the next year, the Communist leadership built the KPA into a formidable offensive force modeled after a Soviet mechanized army. The Chinese released Korean veterans from the People's Liberation Army, while the Soviets provided armaments. By 1950 the North Koreans enjoyed substantial advantages over the South in every category of equipment. After another Kim visit to Moscow in March–April 1950, Stalin approved an invasion.

HOSTILITIES BEGIN

Early in the morning of June 25, 1950, the armed forces of the Democratic People's Republic of Korea smashed across the 38th parallel of latitude in an invasion of the Republic of Korea that achieved complete surprise. Although attacks came all along the border, the major North Korean thrust was in the west of the Korean peninsula, toward Seoul, the capital of South Korea.

South Korea's army was unable to stem the onslaught. By June 28, Seoul had fallen, and across the peninsula, everywhere south of the Han River, the shattered remnants of South Korea's army were in full retreat.

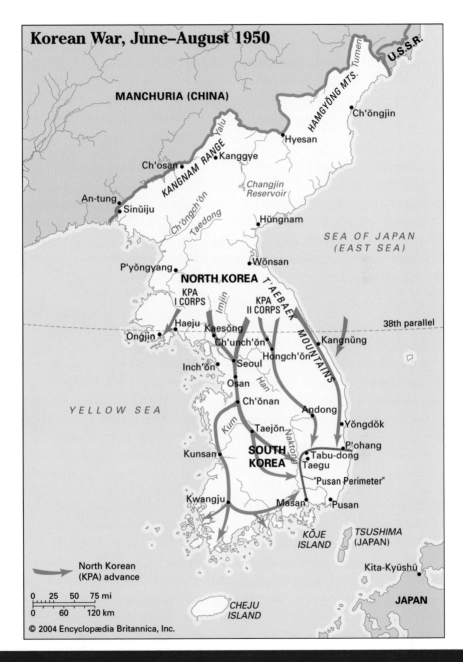

Korean War, June–August 1950

MANCHURIA (CHINA)

HAMGYŎNG MTS.

Tumen

U.S.S.R.

Ch'ŏngjin

Yalu

KANGNAM RANGE

Hyesan

Ch'osan

Kanggye

An-tung

Sinŭiju

Ch'ŏngch'ŏn

Taedong

Changjin Reservoir

Hŭngnam

SEA OF JAPAN (EAST SEA)

P'yŏngyang

Wŏnsan

NORTH KOREA

KPA I CORPS

Imjin

TAEBAEK

KPA II CORPS

38th parallel

Haeju

Kaesŏng

Kangnŭng

Ongjin

Ch'unch'ŏn

MOUNTAINS

Inch'ŏn

Seoul

Hongch'ŏn

Osan

Han

Ch'ŏnan

Andong

YELLOW SEA

Taejŏn

Yŏngdŏk

Kum

Naktong

P'ohang

Kunsan

SOUTH KOREA

Tabu-dong

Taegu

"Pusan Perimeter"

Kwangju

Masan

Pusan

KŎJE ISLAND

TSUSHIMA (JAPAN)

North Korean (KPA) advance

Kita-Kyūshū

0 25 50 75 mi

0 60 120 km

CHEJU ISLAND

JAPAN

© 2004 Encyclopædia Britannica, Inc.

In the beginning stages of the war, North Korean forces overran much of South Korea. South Korean forces along with U.S. troops retreated to a small area, called the Pusan Perimeter, on Korea's southeastern tip.

THE UNITED NATIONS REACTION

Within hours after the invasion of South Korea began, the United Nations Security Council called for an immediate cease-fire and the withdrawal of North Korean forces from South Korea. North Korea ignored the resolution. Two days later the Security Council urged United Nations members to assist South Korea in repelling its invaders. Both resolutions passed because the Soviet Union was boycotting Security Council meetings. Had the Soviet delegate been present, he surely would have vetoed the measures.

In response, 16 nations sent troops to the aid of South Korea. The United States sent an army; Great Britain, a division; and other nations, lesser units. The heaviest burden of the war, however, was borne by South Korea itself. Its army reached a peak strength of some 400,000 men. It maintained that strength only by a steady

flow of hastily trained replacements, and sustained an estimated 850,000 combat casualties. The United States Army in Korea ultimately numbered some

South Korean troops march through a destroyed village. At the beginning of the war, North Korean forces significantly outnumbered South Korean troops, but UN and U.S. aid helped secure victories for South Korea.

300,000 men, supported by about 50,000 Marine,
Air Force, and Navy combatants.

THE UNITED STATES REACTION

The United States reacted even more quickly
than did the United Nations. Upon hearing of the
North Korean attack, President Harry S. Truman
directed General of the Army Douglas MacArthur,
commander of the United States occupation forces in
Japan, to insure the safe evacuation of United States
civilians and to supply weapons and ammunition to
South Korea.

On June 26, United States air and naval forces
were directed to support South Korean ground units.
The commitment of United States ground forces
was authorized after General MacArthur inspected
the battlefront. The ground forces available to
General MacArthur in Japan were four understrength
Army divisions composed largely of inexperienced,
undertrained men and lacking in heavy weapons.

Early in July the United Nations asked the
United States to appoint a commander for all United
Nations forces in Korea. President Truman named
General MacArthur. Soon thereafter, South Korea
placed its forces under the United Nations command.

After the fall of Seoul, North Korea's forces
paused briefly to regroup, then resumed their
southward drive. South Korea's army resisted bravely
but was pushed back steadily. Three United States
divisions sent to its aid were committed in small
units. They too were driven into retreat.

By late July the remnants of South Korea's army and the United States units had been pressed into a small, roughly rectangular area surrounding the port of Pusan at the southeastern tip of Korea. Here, defending a perimeter roughly 150 miles (240 kilometers) long, the United Nations forces finally were able to hold as reinforcements poured in.

Armored vehicles are transported on railroad cars to the war front in Pusan. UN forces defended the area during the Battle of the Pusan Perimeter between August and September 1950.

MASTERSTROKE REVERSES COURSE OF WAR

While North Korea continued to hurl furious but ineffective attacks at the Pusan Perimeter, General MacArthur readied the counterstroke that was to reverse the course of the war—an amphibious assault in his enemy's rear at the port city of Inch'ŏn, southwest of Seoul. MacArthur did not believe that he could win the war without an amphibious landing deep behind enemy lines, and he had started to think about a landing as early as July. For the core of his landing force, he and the Joint Chiefs of Staff selected the 1st Marine Division and the Eighth Army's remaining infantry division, the 7th. As the force developed, it also included South Korean marine and infantry units and an assortment of U.S. support troops. The entire force was designated X Corps and was commanded by Major General Edward M. Almond, MacArthur's chief of staff.

On September 15, 1950, a Marine division swarmed ashore at Inch'ŏn after preparatory bombardment by aircraft and naval guns. An Army division followed. Simultaneously, the Eighth Army—by now a well-equipped and cohesive force—broke out of the Pusan Perimeter. Although bloody fighting ensued, Seoul was recaptured within a few days. Thereafter the North Korean army—its supply line severed and its principal withdrawal route blocked by the capture of Seoul—rapidly collapsed. By October 1 its remnants, utterly destroyed as a fighting force, had retreated above the 38th parallel. The amazement created by the sudden appearance of the X Corps at Inch'ŏn added more luster to MacArthur's already brilliant career, and

U.S. Marines watch the Battle at Inch'on from off shore. The success of the Marine operation ended the Battle of the Pusan Perimeter and gave UN forces a much-needed edge over North Korean forces.

INCH'ŎN LANDING

General MacArthur had started to think about a landing somewhere behind enemy lines in early July 1950, and on August 12 he ordered his staff to prepare for an amphibious landing at Inch'ŏn, the port outlet of Seoul, located on Korea's west coast.

The Joint Chiefs of Staff were at first opposed to such a landing. They feared that because of the grave situation at the Pusan Perimeter, MacArthur would not be able to hold out enough units to fight elsewhere and might be defeated in both places. In addition, they did not think the plans could be ready in time, and they doubted that Inch'ŏn was the right place for a landing. Beaches could be used for only 6 hours out of each 24. The only approach to the port was through a narrow, tortuous channel, blocked by a key harbor defense site, Wolmi Island, and the port facilities of Inch'ŏn were inadequate for supporting a major operation. However, MacArthur knew that practically the entire KPA had been committed to the assaults on Pusan. The Inch'ŏn-Seoul area was weakly held, and nowhere else were the North Koreans' lines of communication so vulnerable or accessible. Furthermore, Seoul, as South Korea's capital, was psychologically important, and MacArthur was determined to reverse the war and restore the United States' damaged prestige as soon as possible.

After a naval gun and aerial bombardment on September 14, U.S. Marines the next day assaulted Wolmi Island. Later that day additional Marine units landed along Inch'ŏn's waterfront. The North Koreans' resistance was not stubborn, and their armored counterattacks over the next two days did little to slow the Marines' advance on Seoul. With Kimpo airfield secured on September 18, the 1st Marine Division put all three of its infantry regiments across the Han River on September 20–25 and captured Seoul. Meanwhile, the 7th Infantry Division went ashore on September 18 and fanned out quickly to the south. On September 26, the day Seoul fell to the Marines, an armored spearhead of the Eighth Army dashing north from the Pusan Perimeter met the 7th Infantry Division at Suwon, south of Seoul. The KPA, completely shattered, had ceased to exist as a cohesive force.

the landing is still considered to be one of the greatest operations in military history.

North Korea had also met disaster in the air. Late in June, United States jet fighters had streaked westward from Japan after a North Korean fighter fired on an American transport. Within two weeks the North Korean air force had ceased to exist, and the United Nations had established an air superiority that it generally was to maintain throughout the war. Even when, later in the war, the Communist forces were supplied with Soviet-built jet fighters equal or superior to the United States aircraft flown by the United Nations, their Chinese—and sometimes Soviet—pilots proved no match for those of the United Nations. In the course of the war, 14 Communist aircraft were shot down for every United Nations plane lost in aerial combat. At sea, under the guns of United States and British warships, North Korea's minuscule navy—a few patrol boats—suffered a fate similar to that of its air force.

CHAPTER TWO

WAR OF ATTRITION

In the United Nations, Communist delegates indicated that North Korea would now be willing to accept restoration of the 38th parallel as the border between the two Koreas. The United States and South Korea, however, decided to forcibly reunite North and South Korea under the government of South Korea. They disbelieved the threat of Communist China that it would intervene if United Nations forces entered North Korea.

NORTH TO DISASTER

United Nations forces began in early October 1950 to press northward. They met only light resistance and by late November had

North Korean and Chinese troops celebrate after a victory over U.S. forces. Chinese forces in North Korea helped drive UN forces back to below the 38th parallel.

captured virtually all of North Korea. At two points, units reached the Yalu River, the border between North Korea and China.

Shortly after the United Nations advance into North Korea began, however, Communist China had secretly begun to infiltrate troops into North Korea. United Nations air patrols detected no sign of them.

United Nations forces had advanced northward in two columns, the Eighth Army in the west and the X Corps in the east, separated by up to 50 miles (80 kilometers) by the central mountain chain of North Korea. Units of both columns were also dispersed and open to attack.

Contacts with Communist Chinese units—some in strength—began in late October and continued into early November. Chinese aircraft—Soviet-built MiG-15 jet fighters—first appeared early in November. However, the United Nations command underestimated the strength of the Chinese forces and misread China's intentions. The command planned a final offensive that would bring all of North Korea under United Nations control, confident that United Nations air power could prevent the Chinese from crossing the Yalu River in sufficient strength to stop the offensive. By this time, however, Chinese Communist troops in North Korea numbered 300,000.

Late in November, across the snow that heralded a harsh North Korean winter, the Chinese struck. Attacking largely at night, the Chinese—though they suffered tremendous casualties—rapidly dislodged the Eighth Army and X Corps.

In the east, X Corps units were withdrawn by sea from the ports of Hŭngnam and Wŏnsan.

Supplies and equipment are loaded onto ships at Hŭngnam, North Korea, after the U.S. retreat from the Chosin Reservoir, December 11, 1950.

BATTLE OF THE CHOSIN RESERVOIR

The Battle of the Chosin Reservoir was part of the Chinese Second Offensive (November–December 1950) to drive the United Nations out of North Korea. The Chosin Reservoir campaign was directed mainly against the 1st Marine Division of the U.S. X Corps, which had disembarked in eastern North Korea and moved inland in severe winter weather to a mountainous area near the reservoir.

The campaign succeeded in forcing the entire X Corps to evacuate to South Korea, but the Chinese did not achieve their particular objective of isolating and destroying the 1st Marine Division. Instead, in a deliberate retrograde movement that has become one of the most-storied exploits in Marine Corps lore, the Marines turned and fought their way down a narrow vulnerable road through several mountain passes and a bridged chasm until they reached transport ships waiting at the coast.

The Chinese have remained vague on their losses in the battle, but their own records and estimates of the United Nations Command (UNC) put the Chinese People's Volunteers Force (CPVF) Ninth Army Group's casualties in the range of 40,000 to 80,000, when one counts combat deaths and wounded plus deaths and incapacity

from the cold. The 1st Marine Division lost 4,385 men to combat and 7,338 to the cold. Other X Corps losses amounted to some 6,000 Americans and Koreans.

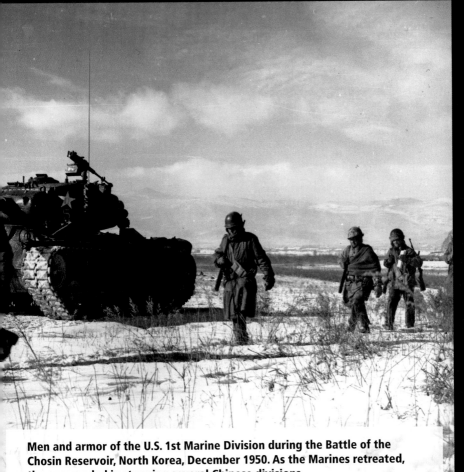

Men and armor of the U.S. 1st Marine Division during the Battle of the Chosin Reservoir, North Korea, December 1950. As the Marines retreated, they succeeded in stopping several Chinese divisions.

Surrounded far inland, the lst Marine Division reached Hŭngnam in one of the great fighting retreats of history. In the west, by land and sea, the Eighth Army also fell back. By the end of December the United Nations forces had been pushed back to a line just south of the 38th parallel. In the face of a renewed Chinese offensive, they withdrew from Seoul and the Han River line early in January 1951.

In the more open terrain of South Korea, the United Nations forces were able to form a fairly continuous line of resistance. They continued to withdraw slowly, exacting a terrible toll of the advancing Chinese, until in mid-January the front stabilized along an undulating line running from the 37th parallel in the west to a point midway between the 37th and 38th parallels in the east.

REUNIFICATION ABANDONED

The entry of China into the war had a heavy impact upon the United States. Draft calls were increased, and more reservists were called to active duty. President Truman declared a state of national emergency, and economic controls were imposed.

Fearing that the wider war with China that would be necessary to reunify Korea would cost too many American lives and raise the risk of nuclear war with the Soviet Union, the United States abandoned the idea of forcibly reuniting the two Koreas. Instead, it decided to accept a rough restoration of the situation that had existed before the war. Although the United Nations declared Communist China an aggressor, it agreed with the new United States policy. United Nations forces would repel China from South Korea but would not seek to retake the north.

By late January 1951 the Eighth Army— reformed and strengthened and incorporating the X Corps—was ready to advance against the now-weakened Chinese and North Korean armies. Thrusts of infantry and armor were supported by the vastly superior United Nations artillery and air power. Where the Communist forces chose to stand, they were slaughtered. In one action alone, 6,000 Chinese men were killed, 25,000 wounded. Seoul was reoccupied by the United Nations in mid-March. By March 31 the battle line stood roughly along the 38th parallel.

Enraged at China's intervention, General MacArthur had dissented vigorously from the new United Nations policy. He wished to press an expanded war against Communist China, including forbidden attacks upon "sanctuaries" above the Yalu River. He made his views public. Believing the general's actions to be both insubordinate and dangerous, President Truman relieved him of his commands in April. General MacArthur was

General Matthew Ridgway *(left, at front)* leads troops along a road. General Ridgway replaced Douglas MacArthur after he was relieved for insubordination.

replaced by Lieut. Gen. Matthew B. Ridgway, who had commanded the Eighth Army in the field since the death of Lieut. Gen. Walton H. Walker in a jeep accident in December 1950. Command of the Eighth Army was passed to Lieut. Gen. James A. Van Fleet.

TRUCE TALKS BEGIN

Above the 38th parallel, the Chinese and North Korean forces once again regrouped. They pursued an approach suggested by Chinese General Peng Dehuai: hold the ground in Korea and conduct a campaign of attrition, attempting to win limited victories against small allied units through violent night attacks and infantry infiltration.

In April and in May, their commanders hurled

them against the United Nations lines. In response, General Van Fleet's forces slowly withdrew, scourging their attackers with superior firepower. When their adversaries were exhausted by massive casualties and supply shortages, the United Nations forces counterattacked. By mid-June, save for a small sector north of Seoul in the west, the United Nations line stood well above the 38th parallel.

Late in June, the Soviet Union indicated that the Communists might be prepared to seek a truce. On June 30, General Ridgway offered to open truce negotiations. North Korea and China accepted.

Truce talks opened on July 10 at Kaesŏng, some 35 miles (56 kilometers) northwest of Seoul. It quickly became apparent that the opposing sides had different goals at the truce table. The United Nations sought only an honorable end to the war. North Korea and China, however, undertook to win in conference what they had been unable to attain on the battlefield. The Communists made every effort to embarrass and humiliate United Nations delegates, to force concessions through intransigence and delay, and to use the conference as a propaganda forum.

Although it was agreed that hostilities were to continue during the truce talks, no more major offensives were conducted during the war. A lull in the fighting developed as the talks opened; both sides used it to strengthen their forces. The Communist buildup was hampered—though not halted—by

A UN convoy can be seen at the "United Nations House" in Kaesŏng, Korea, during early Korean War armistice talks, 1951.

United Nations naval and air forces.

Late in August, the Communists broke off the truce talks. General Van Fleet promptly launched a limited offensive to straighten and improve the United Nations lines. By mid-October, defeated again, the Communists offered to reopen the truce talks.

The meeting site was moved to P'anmunjŏm, some 5 miles (8 kilometers) east of Kaesŏng. Here the armistice talks were to drag on, with intermittent recesses, for another year and a half, stalling repeatedly over such issues as the establishment of a truce line and the repatriation of prisoners. Along

James Van Fleet (*third from right*), seen here with a battalion from Colombia (the only South American country to participate in the war), was promoted to general in July 1951, not long before he launched the offensive that would help reopen truce talks with the Communists.

DEMILITARIZED ZONE

A demilitarized zone (DMZ) was created during armistice talks by pulling back the respective forces 1.2 miles (2 kilometers) along each side of the boundary at the 38th Parallel. It runs for about 150 miles (240 kilometers) across the peninsula, from the mouth of the Han River on the west coast to a little south of the North Korean town of Kosŏng on the east coast. Located within the DMZ is the "truce village" of P'anmunjŏm, about 5 miles (8 kilometers) east of Kaesŏng. It was the site of peace discussions during the Korean War and has since been the location of various conferences over issues related to North and South Korea, their allies, and the UN.

The areas north and south of the DMZ are heavily fortified, and both sides maintain large contingents of troops there. Over the years there have been occasional incidents and minor skirmishes but no significant conflicts. Since the end of the Korean War the DMZ, which was once farmland, has lain almost untouched and, to a large extent, has reverted to nature. In mid-2007 limited cargo-train service was resumed across the zone.

Military vehicles cross the 38th parallel during the Korean War.

the front, meanwhile, the fighting settled into a
modernized version of the grinding trench warfare
of World War I.

A LONG AND UNEASY TRUCE

In order to maintain the military pressure that
seemed essential to serious negotiations, the
United Nations insisted that the truce line be the
line of contact between
the opposing armies
at the time the truce
was signed. Finally,
a line was agreed
upon. Finally, too, the
Communists agreed
that prisoners who did
not wish to return to
their homelands did
not have to. At first,
they had insisted that
the United Nations
return, by force if
necessary, all the
Communist prisoners it
held. Nearly half of all
the prisoners held by
the United Nations—
and three quarters of

the Chinese—did not wish to return to Communist rule. The truce agreement was finally signed July 27, 1953, and that day, at 10:00 pm, Korean time, the guns fell silent along the blood-soaked main line of resistance.

The conclusion of the cease-fire had probably been hastened by events outside of Korea. First, General of the Army Dwight D. Eisenhower, who succeeded Truman as president of the United States in January 1953, had hinted broadly that military pressure might be sharply increased if the fighting

UN delegate Lieut. Gen. William K. Harrison, Jr. (*seated left*), and Korean People's Army and Chinese People's Volunteers delegate Gen. Nam Il (*seated right*) sign the Korean War armistice agreement at P'anmunjŏm, Korea, July 27, 1953.

did not end soon. Second, the death in March 1953 of Soviet dictator Joseph Stalin caused a general turning inward of the Communist world.

After the cease-fire, the opposing forces each withdrew 1.25 miles (2 kilometers) from the truce line. The armistice agreement had provided for a conference to seek a permanent peace, but—in the face of Communist intransigence—it was delayed for many years. United States troops remained in South Korea, and heavily armed North Korean and South Korean forces still faced each other across a narrow demilitarized zone. Truce violations remain common.

CHAPTER THREE

POLITICAL LEADERS

The conflict between the Democratic People's Republic of Korea (North Korea) and the Republic of Korea (South Korea) was at the center of the Korean War. However, the heavy involvement of the Soviet Union, China, and the United States, amongst others, elevated the conflict to one of global scale. Existing Cold War tensions between the United States and the world's Communist powers became primary considerations for leaders such as Harry Truman, Joseph Stalin, and Mao Zedong and informed their dealings with the leaders of North and South Korea. As the political architects, their management of the conflict in large part determined the course both of the Korean War and later world history.

SYNGMAN RHEE

(1875–1965)

Syngman Rhee was born in Whanghae Province, Korea, on April 26, 1875. After a traditional classical education, he entered a Methodist school, where he learned English. In 1896 he

Syngman Rhee (*left*) stands with his wife, Franziska Donner, and General James Van Fleet in South Korea.

joined a political group organized to fight for Korean sovereignty and civil rights. He was imprisoned from 1898 to 1904, and on his release he went to the United States. Rhee was the first Korean to earn a Ph.D. from an American university—Princeton, in 1910. He returned briefly to Korea, but his hostility to Japanese rule caused him to go back to the United States in 1912.

Rhee was president of a provisional government in exile from 1919 to 1941 and continued his campaign for Korean independence. Rhee returned to Korea in 1945 and built a political organization supported by strong-arm squads and the police. Moderate leaders were assassinated, and his party won the elections in South Korea in 1948. As president, Rhee assumed dictatorial powers, purged the National Assembly, and outlawed the opposition Progressive Party, whose leader was executed for treason. He controlled the appointment of mayors, village headmen, and chiefs of police. He even defied the United Nations (UN) during the Korean War.

Hoping that UN forces would continue to fight and eventually unite North and South Korea under one government, Rhee hindered the truce talks by ordering the release in June 1953 of some 25,000 anti-Communist North Korean prisoners. (Under the agreed-upon truce settlement, these men were to have been repatriated to North Korea.) Stunned, the Communists broke off the negotiations and renewed their attack, largely ignoring the UN forces and concentrating their fire on Rhee's South Korean troops. Having made their point, the Communists then resumed negotiations, and a truce settlement was speedily signed.

He was reelected in 1952, 1956, and 1960, but a month after the last election charges of vote fraud provoked student-led demonstrations. The April Revolution resulted in heavy casualties and forced his resignation. Rhee went into exile in Hawaii. He died in Honolulu on July 19, 1965.

JOSEPH STALIN
(1878–1953)

Joseph Stalin was born in Gori, a village in Georgia, then part of the Russian Empire, on December 18, 1878. After attending a church school, he studied at a seminary but was expelled for revolutionary activity in 1899. He joined an underground revolutionary group and sided with the Bolshevik faction of the Russian Social-Democratic Workers' Party in 1903. A disciple of Vladimir Lenin, he served in minor party posts and was appointed to the first Bolshevik Central Committee (1912). He remained active behind the scenes and in exile (1913–17) until the Russian Revolution of 1917 brought the Bolsheviks to power.

Stalin's original Georgian name was Ioseb Dzhugashvili, but in 1912 he adopted the name Stalin (from the Russian *stal*, or "steel"). He served as commissar for nationalities and for state control in the Bolshevik government (1917–23). He was a member of the Politburo, and in 1922 he became secretary-general of the party's Central Committee. After Lenin's death (1924), Stalin overcame his rivals, including Leon Trotsky, Grigory Zinovyev, Lev Kamenev, Nikolay Bukharin, and Aleksey Rykov, and took control of Soviet politics. In 1928 he inaugurated the Five-Year Plans that radically altered Soviet economic and social structures and resulted in the deaths of many millions. In the 1930s he contrived to eliminate threats to his power through the purge trials and through widespread secret executions and persecution. In World War II he signed the German-Soviet Nonaggression Pact (1939), attacked Finland, and annexed parts of eastern Europe to strengthen his western frontiers. When Germany invaded Russia (1941), Stalin took control of military operations. He allied Russia with Britain and the U.S.; at the Tehran,

Yalta, and Potsdam conferences, he demonstrated his negotiating skill.

After the war he consolidated Soviet power in eastern Europe and built up the Soviet Union as a world military power. Far from continuing his wartime alliance with the United States and Great Britain, Stalin now regarded these countries—and especially the United States—as the arch-enemies that he needed after Hitler's death. He continued his repressive political measures to control internal dissent; increasingly paranoid, he was preparing to mount another purge after the so-called Doctors' Plot when he died on March 5, 1953. Noted for bringing the Soviet Union into world prominence, at terrible cost to his own people, he left a legacy of repression and fear as well as industrial and military power. In 1956 Stalin and his personality cult were denounced by Nikita Khrushchev.

HARRY S. TRUMAN
(1884–1972)

The man who was to guide the United States through some of its most trying times was born May 8, 1884, at Lamar, Missouri. Harry Truman was the son of John Anderson Truman, a cattle trader, and Martha Young Truman.

Truman worked at various jobs before serving with distinction in World War I. He became a partner in a Kansas City haberdashery; when the business failed, he entered Democratic Party politics with the help of Thomas Pendergast. He was elected county judge (1922–24), and he later became presiding judge of the county court (1926–34). His reputation for honesty and good management gained him bipartisan support.

In the U.S. Senate (1935–45), Truman led a committee that exposed fraud in defense production. In 1944 he was chosen to replace the incumbent Henry Wallace as the Democratic Party vice presidential nominee, and he won election with Pres. Franklin D. Roosevelt. After only 82 days as vice president, he became president on Roosevelt's death (April 1945). He quickly made final arrangements for the San Francisco charter-writing meeting of the UN, helped arrange Germany's unconditional surrender on May 8, which ended World War II in Europe, and in July attended the Potsdam Conference. The Pacific war ended officially on September 2, after he ordered atomic bombs dropped on Hiroshima and Nagasaki; his justification was a report that 500,000 U.S. troops would be lost in a conventional invasion of Japan.

On June 25, 1950, war broke out in Korea. This was a great personal blow to President Truman. He had often said he wanted more than anything else to be regarded by historians as a president who brought peace to the world. Truman ordered the United States military forces to support the United Nations "police action" in Korea. On December 16 he declared a state of national emergency to help prepare the United States for a possible "all-out" war with Communism.

The nation's foreign policies overshadowed all other political issues in 1951. After long debate the

Senate voted to send four additional Army divisions to Europe as part of the North Atlantic Treaty Organization (NATO) forces. There they came under the overall Allied command of Gen. Dwight D. Eisenhower.

In Korea, American and other United Nations troops were fighting a huge force of Communists— the North Korean army had Chinese "volunteers." President Truman insisted on confining the fight to Korea. The supreme commander in the Far East, Gen. Douglas MacArthur, and others wanted to strike directly at China in an effort to win a quick victory. On April 11 Truman relieved MacArthur and appointed Gen. Matthew Ridgway top commander in the Far East.

Ridgway later became supreme commander, Allied Powers in Europe, when Eisenhower asked to be relieved of that post by June 1, 1952. Eisenhower

President Harry Truman (*left*) meets with General Douglas MacArthur. Truman relieved MacArthur of his position as supreme commander in the Far East in 1951 for MacArthur's disagreement with U.S. policy in Korea.

then came home to seek the Republican presidential nomination.

On the home front the nation worked to rearm itself and its Allies. Before the outbreak of fighting in Korea, the United States was devoting 6 percent of its industrial production to national defense. By 1952 it had climbed to 20 percent of all production in the midst of a growing peacetime economic expansion. The cost of living, by the summer of 1951, had soared to more than 185 percent of the base average of 1935–39, and prices had climbed about 9 percent since 1950.

President Truman refused to seek reelection in 1952, and the Democratic nomination went to Governor Adlai E. Stevenson of Illinois. The candidate for the Republican party was Gen. Dwight D. Eisenhower.

Eisenhower was inaugurated president on January 20, 1953, and Harry Truman retired to his home in Independence, Missouri. After his death on December 26, 1972, Harry Truman was buried in Independence in the courtyard of the library built in his name.

DWIGHT D. EISENHOWER
(1890–1969)

Born on October 14, 1890, in Denison, Texas, Dwight Eisenhower was the third of seven sons of David Jacob and Ida Elizabeth (Stover) Eisenhower. In the spring of 1891 the Eisenhowers left Denison and returned to Abilene, Kansas, where their forebears had settled as part of a Mennonite colony.

Eisenhower graduated from West Point in 1915, then served in the Panama Canal Zone (1922–24) and in the Philippines under Douglas MacArthur (1935–39). In World War II Gen. George Marshall appointed him to the army's war-plans division (1941), then chose him to command U.S. forces in Europe (1942). After planning the invasions of North Africa, Sicily, and Italy, he was appointed supreme commander of Allied forces (1943). He planned the Normandy Campaign (1944) and the conduct of the war in Europe until the German surrender (1945). Eisenhower was promoted to five-star general (1944) and was named army chief of staff in 1945. He served as president of Columbia University from 1948 until being appointed supreme commander of NATO in 1951.

Both Democrats and Republicans courted Eisenhower as a presidential candidate; in 1952, as the Republican candidate, he defeated Adlai Stevenson with the largest popular vote to that time.

Throughout the campaign he called for a firm, middle-of-the-road policy in both foreign and domestic affairs. Eisenhower urged economy and honesty in government and promised to visit Korea to explore the possibilities for ending the Korean War. Many Republicans, including California senator and Eisenhower running mate Richard Nixon, spoke of pro-Communist disloyalty within the Truman administration and called for stringent antisubversive measures. In an effort to find a solution to the stalemated Korean War he dramatically promised: "I shall go to Korea." The Eisenhower-Nixon ticket won handily, carrying 39 states, winning the electoral vote 442 to 89, and collecting more than 33 million popular votes.

Foreign affairs—particularly the growing Cold War rivalry between the United States and the Soviet Union—drew much of Eisenhower's attention. The Korean War was a key conflict in the early years of the Cold War. It had begun in 1950 when Communist North Korea, backed by the Soviets, invaded South Korea, a democracy supported by the United States.

Four weeks into his presidency, Eisenhower honored his boldest campaign promise by making a special trip to Korea. In a closely guarded visit he toured the battlefront studying

Dwight D. Eisenhower (*far left*) reviews troops in Korea. Eisenhower visited Korea soon after he assumed the office of president, which he had promised to do during his campaign.

the possibilities of an honorable peace settlement. In July 1953 the president formally announced the signing of a truce. He warned, however, that the United States must remain on guard against other acts of Communist aggression. This warning was underscored in August when the Soviet Union revealed that it had developed an H-bomb.

The increasing threat of communist expansionism in the Far East led to a meeting of eight countries in Manila. In September 1954 these countries formed the Southeast Asia Treaty Organization (SEATO) for the collective defense of the area. Member countries were the United States, Australia, France, Great Britain, New Zealand, Pakistan, the Philippines, and Thailand.

Eisenhower defeated Stevenson again in 1956 in an even larger landslide. His policy of support for Middle Eastern countries facing Communist aggression, enunciated in the Eisenhower Doctrine, was a continuation of the containment policy adopted by the Harry Truman administration. He sent federal troops to Little Rock, Arkansas, to enforce integration of a city high school (1957). When the Soviet Union launched *Sputnik I* (1957), he was criticized for failing to develop the U.S. space program; he responded by creating NASA (1958). In his last weeks in office the U.S. broke diplomatic relations with Cuba.

After a long period of illness and a hospital confinement of almost a year, Eisenhower died of heart failure on March 28, 1969, at the Walter Reed General Hospital in Washington.

DEAN ACHESON
(1893–1971)

U.S. statesman Dean G. Acheson served as secretary of state from 1949 to 1953 and was an adviser to four presidents. Noted as the principal creator of U.S. foreign policy in the Cold War period following World War II, he helped to create the Western alliance in opposition to the Soviet Union and other communist nations.

Dean Gooderham Acheson was born on April 11, 1893, in Middletown, Connecticut. A graduate of Yale University and of Harvard Law School, he served as a law clerk for Supreme Court Justice Louis D. Brandeis. In 1921 Acheson joined a law firm in Washington, D.C. His first government post was in the administration of Franklin D. Roosevelt as undersecretary of the Treasury in 1933; Acheson entered the Department of State in 1941 as an assistant secretary and was undersecretary from 1945 to 1947.

One of Acheson's first responsibilities in 1945 was to secure Senate approval for U.S. membership in the United Nations. About that same time he became a convinced anti-Communist, a position that was the dominant influence on his later conduct of foreign policy. Believing that the Soviet Union sought expansion in the Middle East, Acheson shaped what came to be known as the Truman Doctrine (1947), pledging immediate military and economic aid to the governments of Greece and Turkey. In the same year he outlined the main points of what became known as the Marshall Plan, a program designed to rehabilitate the economies of numerous western and southern European countries in order to create stable conditions in which democratic institutions could survive.

President Harry S. Truman appointed Acheson secretary of state in January 1949. In that role Acheson promoted the formation of the North Atlantic Treaty Organization (NATO), the first peacetime defensive alliance entered into by the United States. Although Acheson was the target of attack by foreign-policy critics for much of his career, he continued to work toward containing Communist expansion and forming a Western alliance.

Despite his strong stance in what he conceived to be a global confrontation with Communism, Acheson was the target of attack by foreign-policy critics within both political parties. His enemies were particularly inflamed when, during the congressional hearings of Senator Joseph R. McCarthy on subversive activities (1949–50), Acheson refused to fire any of his State Department subordinates. His most widely publicized remark was, "I will not turn my back on Alger Hiss"—a former State Department officer later convicted of perjury in denying that he had engaged in espionage in the 1930s.

Demands for Acheson's resignation increased after the entry of Communist China into the Korean War. The storm of public controversy erupted more violently after the president removed General Douglas MacArthur as commander of forces in Korea. Acheson subsequently established the policies of nonrecognition of China and aid to the Nationalist regime of General Chiang Kai-shek on Taiwan; later he also supported U.S. aid to the French colonial regime in Indochina.

After leaving office Acheson returned to private law practice but continued to serve as foreign-policy adviser to successive presidents. His account of his years in the Department of State, *Present at the Creation*, won the Pulitzer Prize in history in 1970, and he was the author of several other works. Acheson died on October 12, 1971, in Sandy Spring, Maryland.

MAO ZEDONG
(1893–1976)

In China Mao Zedong is remembered and revered as the greatest of revolutionaries. His achievements as ruler, however, have been deservedly downgraded because he was among the worst of politicians. He knew well how to make a revolution, but once in power he could not put his love of revolution aside for the sake of governing.

Mao was born on December 6, 1893, in Shaoshan, Hunan Province. His father was a peasant who had become successful as a grain dealer. Mao's schooling was intermittent. During the Revolution of 1911–12 he served in the army for six months. After that he drifted for a while without goals, but he managed to graduate from the First Provincial Normal School in Changsha in 1918. He then went to Peking University, where he became embroiled in the revolutionary May Fourth Movement. This movement marked the decisive turn in Chinese revolutionary thought in favor of Marxist Communism as a solution to China's problems.

In 1921 Mao helped found the Chinese Communist Party. He was at that time a school principal in Hunan. Two years later, when the Communists forged an alliance with Sun Yat-sen's Nationalist Party (the Kuomintang), he left work to become a full-time revolutionary. It was at this time that Mao discovered the great potential of the peasant class for making revolution. This realization led him to the brilliant strategy he used to win control of China: gain control of the countryside and encircle the cities.

The Communists and the Nationalists coexisted in an uneasy relationship until the end of World War II. The Nationalist leader after 1925 was Chiang Kai-shek, who was determined to rule China. He never trusted the Communists, and at times he persecuted them. Mao's first wife was executed by the Nationalists in 1930.

The Chinese Soviet Republic was founded in November 1931 in Jiangxi Province. In 1934 Mao and his forces were driven out, and they went northward in what is known as the Long March. By 1935, however, the

Communists and Nationalists forged a united front against the Japanese. Rivalry persisted, but the front held until 1945. The revolution that then began ended in 1949 with the Communists victorious.

A delegate of the North Korean People's Army presents Mao Zedong with flowers. Chinese forces were instrumental in many North Korean victories during the Korean War.

In addition to his problems with the Nationalists, Mao's dealings with the Soviet Union's Joseph Stalin were always uneasy. Stalin grew wary of a competing Communist power of China's size on the Soviet borders. Mao eventually came to regard the Soviets as revisionists and felt they were traitors to the cause of world revolution.

Nevertheless, when the Communists did take power in China, both Mao and Stalin had to make the best of the situation. In December 1949 Mao, now chairman of the People's Republic of China—which he had proclaimed on October 1—traveled to Moscow, where, after two months of arduous negotiations, he succeeded in persuading Stalin to sign a treaty of mutual assistance accompanied by limited economic aid. Before the Chinese had time to profit from the resources made available for economic development, however, they found themselves dragged into the Korean War in support of the Moscow-oriented regime in P'yŏngyang. Only after this baptism of fire did Stalin, according to Mao, begin to have confidence in him and believe he was not first and foremost a Chinese nationalist.

Despite these tensions with Moscow, the policies of the People's Republic of China in its early years were in very many respects based, as Mao later said, on "copying from the Soviets." While Mao and his comrades had experience in guerrilla warfare, in mobilization of the peasants in the countryside, and in political administration at the grass roots, they had no firsthand knowledge of running a state or of large-scale economic development. In such circumstances the Soviet Union provided the only available model. A five-year plan was therefore drawn up under Soviet guidance; it was put into effect in 1953 and included Soviet technical assistance and a number of complete industrial plants. Yet, within two years, Mao had taken steps that were to lead to the breakdown of the political and ideological alliance with Moscow.

Mao's title as ruler of China was chairman of the People's Republic. For the first five years he rarely appeared in public and seemed to be only a ceremonial figure. He never achieved the total control in China that Stalin did in the Soviet Union. Many of his comrades were influential in directing policy, often in ways with which Mao disagreed. In 1955 he emerged from isolation determined to play the decisive role in economic policy and political restructuring.

Failing to gain the allegiance of the intellectuals, he turned to the masses with a program called the Great Leap Forward. While not a complete economic disaster, it had severe consequences. After it disrupted both city and countryside, he was forced to retreat from his policies in favor of his opponents. To counter opposition he launched the Great Proletarian Cultural Revolution, urged on by his radical wife, Jiang Qing. This vast upheaval wrecked the Communist Party bureaucracy, paralyzed education and research, and left the economy almost a shambles.

Only slowly did China begin to recover. By then Mao was old and ill. Other, more moderate hands guided policy. Zhou Enlai seemed to emerge as the nation's real leader when relations were reestablished with the United States.

Mao's personality cult remained strong until his death on September 9, 1976. Shortly afterward, however, a power struggle was under way. Members of the party who had been purged by the Cultural Revolution returned to govern China. Chief among them was Deng Xiaoping.

KIM IL-SUNG
(1912–94)

When a separate North Korean government was established in 1948, Kim Il-Sung of the dominant Korean Workers' (Communist) Party became its leader. The first premier of North Korea, he became president under a new constitution in 1972. He ruled North Korea as a dictator until his death in 1994.

Kim Song-Ju was born on April 15, 1912, near P'yŏngyang, Korea. He joined the Korean Communist Party in 1931. During the 1930s he led armed resistance to the Japanese occupation of Korea and took the name Kim

Il-Sung from an earlier anti-Japanese guerrilla fighter. After leading a Korean force in the Soviet army during World War II, he returned in 1945 to establish a

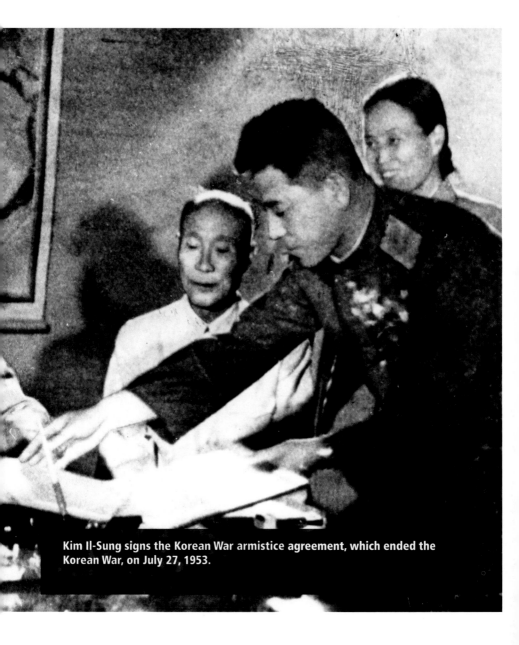

Kim Il-Sung signs the Korean War armistice agreement, which ended the Korean War, on July 27, 1953.

Communist government under Soviet auspices in what would become North Korea.

In 1950 Kim Il-Sung made an unsuccessful attempt to extend his rule to South Korea, thereby starting the Korean War. With Chinese aid, he then repelled a subsequent invasion of North Korea by U.S. troops and other forces of the United Nations. The war ended in a stalemate in 1953.

As head of state, Kim eliminated all political opposition and became his country's absolute ruler. The twin goals of his regime were industrialization and the reunification of the Korean peninsula under North Korean rule. North Korea's state-run economy grew rapidly in the 1950s and '60s but eventually faltered, with shortages of food occurring by the early '90s. In his foreign policy Kim allied North Korea with the Soviet Union and China and remained hostile to South Korea and the United States. His rule went unchallenged for 46 years largely because of a propaganda system that promoted a personality cult centered on Kim as Korea's "Great Leader."

In 1994 Kim's desire to start a nuclear weapons program led to urgent international efforts to avoid war and to negotiate reunification. He died on July 8, 1994, just weeks before the talks were to begin. He was succeeded by his son, Kim Jong Il. A revised constitution introduced in 1998 enshrined Kim Il-Sung as "eternal president of the republic."

CHAPTER FOUR

MILITARY FIGURES

Although the Korean War was not likely to result in a complete military victory for either side, the importance of military leadership, strategy, and sacrifice to the conflict cannot be overstated. Military leaders were instrumental in setting precedents in the new age of limited war. Key military engagements, such as those at Inch'ŏn and at the Chosin Reservoir, asserted the force of the United States and its allies against the world's major Communist authorities. For its part, China emerged as a rising global power.

DOUGLAS MACARTHUR
(1880–1964)

A symbol of American determination and fighting ability, Gen. Douglas MacArthur played a major role in the ability of the United States to prepare for action in the early days of World War II. On Dec. 7, 1941, Japanese bombers attacked a U.S. military base at Pearl Harbor in Hawaii without warning. Japan's troops then swept down through East Asia and the Pacific with frightening swiftness. MacArthur, who was in the Philippines at the time, helped stall the advancing wave, an effort that proved crucial to the war effort.

Douglas MacArthur was born on Jan. 26, 1880, on an Army reservation in Little Rock, Arkansas. His father, Gen. Arthur MacArthur, served with distinction in the American Civil and Spanish-American wars and was military governor of the Philippines under President William McKinley.

Young MacArthur graduated from the United States Military Academy at West Point, New York, in 1903 with the highest scholastic record achieved by any cadet in 25 years. When the United States entered World War I, he helped organize the Rainbow Division and served with distinction. After the war he was appointed superintendent of West Point. Only 39 years old, he was the youngest superintendent in the history of the academy. At 50 he was made chief of staff of the Army by President Herbert Hoover. He became the youngest full general in United States history.

For the next five years MacArthur tried, with little success, to get the Army mechanized. He was then assigned to organize the defense of the Philippines. In 1937 he retired from the service but continued his work in the Philippines. President Manuel Quezon gave him the rank of field marshal.

In July 1941 MacArthur was recalled to active service as commander of the United States forces in the Far East. That December the Japanese bombed Pearl Harbor. They launched another attack on the Philippines, but MacArthur stood firm. Under his command 12,000 American and 35,000 Filipino troops put up fierce resistance. Besieged on the Bataan peninsula, they beat back a vastly superior Japanese invasion force. The stand made by MacArthur's men delayed the Japanese "timetable of conquest" and gave the United States time to assess the situation.

Meanwhile the island continent of Australia was threatened with invasion. As the last major base in the Pacific for the Allied forces, Australia's defenses had to be bolstered.

On Feb. 22, 1942, President Franklin D. Roosevelt sent a secret message to MacArthur commanding him to break through the Japanese lines and go to Australia. There he was to take command of Allied forces in the Southwest Pacific.

MacArthur transferred his Philippine command to Gen. Jonathan M. Wainwright. On the night of March 11, MacArthur, his wife and son, and members of his staff ran the Japanese blockade in four torpedo boats. The Philippines fell to Japan a few months later, but MacArthur's promise to the Filipinos, "I shall return," gave them courage through more than three years of Japanese occupation.

MacArthur was to keep that promise. On October 20, 1944, he landed with his forces on Leyte, one of the Philippine islands. Less than a year later, on Sept. 2, 1945, MacArthur, as commander in chief in the Pacific, accepted Japan's surrender. He then directed the occupation of Japan.

At the outbreak of hostilities in Korea in 1950, MacArthur became commander of the United Nations forces. After stemming the North Korean advance near Pusan, he carried out a daring landing at Inch'ŏn in September and advanced into North Korea in October as the North Korean army rapidly

General Douglas MacArthur (*seated*) observes the X Corps during the Inch'on landing, which helped turn the tide of the Korean War. The commander of the X Corps, General Edward Almond, can be seen at the far right.

disintegrated. In November, however, massive Chinese forces attacked MacArthur's divided army above the 38th parallel and forced it to retreat

to below Seoul. Two months later MacArthur's troops returned to the offensive, driving into North Korea again.

In 1951 he urged the opening of a "second front" in China. On April 11, 1951, Pres. Harry S. Truman relieved MacArthur of his commands because of the general's insubordination and unwillingness to conduct a limited war. Returning to the United States for the first time since before World War II, MacArthur at first received widespread popular support; the excitement waned after a publicized Senate investigation of his dismissal.

MacArthur and his family returned to the United States in 1951. In a speech before Congress he announced his retirement from active military service with the now famous line from an old ballad, "Old soldiers never die—they just fade away." In 1952 he became chairman of the board of a large corporation and was the keynote speaker at the Republican national convention.

In December 1944 MacArthur was made a five-star general of the Army. He died in Washington, D.C., on April 5, 1964, and was buried in the MacArthur Memorial in Norfolk, Virginia.

WALTON WALKER
(1889–1950)

Walton Walker attended the Virginia Military Institute (1907–08) and then entered the United States Military Academy at West Point, New York, graduating in 1912 and receiving his commission in the infantry. He took part in the occupation of Veracruz, Mexico, in April 1914, and received a number of routine garrison assignments. With the entry of the United States into World War I, he went to France in April 1918 with a machine-gun battalion, seeing action in the Saint-Mihiel and Meuse-Argonne offensives.

Following the occupation period, Walton spent the next two decades of his military career in various

posts, including serving as instructor at the Field
Artillery School, Fort Sill, Oklahoma, at the Infantry
School, Fort Benning, Georgia, and at West Point.
In 1936 he graduated from the Army War College
at Carlisle Barracks, Pennsylvania, and in 1937–40
he was attached to the War Plans Division of the
General Staff in Washington, D.C. From 1941 to
1943 (during which time the United States entered
World War II), he was given command, in succession,
of an infantry division, an armored brigade, an
armored division, and finally an armored corps.
His IV Armored Corps, based at Fort Campbell,
Kentucky, trained at the Desert Training Center on
the California-Arizona border, originally established
to prepare armored units for combat in North Africa.
It was redesignated the XX Corps in October 1943
and was ordered to England in February 1944. The
XX Corps landed in France in July 1944 and, as an
element of Gen. George S. Patton's Third Army,
captured Reims, crossed the Moselle River, reduced
the fortress complex at Metz, and broke through the
Siegfried Line, earning the nickname "Ghost Corps"
for the speed of its advance.

After postwar assignments in the United
States, in September 1948 Walker was transferred
to Japan to command the Eighth Army, which
constituted the ground arm of Gen. Douglas
MacArthur's Far East Command. Following the
North Korean invasion of South Korea on June 25,
1950, Eighth Army headquarters transferred to
Taegu, South Korea. Walker also received command

Walton Walker (*left*) walks with General Douglas MacArthur during the Korean War. Walker's skilled command of the Eighth Army ultimately allowed UN forces to push north and take North Korea's capital city.

of the Republic of Korea Army (ROKA) and of other
United Nations forces as they arrived.

With most of his U.S. units understrength, his
ROKA forces demoralized, and tactical air support
insufficient, Walker was forced to fight a stubborn withdrawal into the southeast corner of the
Korean peninsula. On July 29 he issued a "stand
or die order," declaring that "there will be no
Dunkirk, there will be no Bataan." Nevertheless,
his defensive line continued to contract until the
arrival of reinforcements, heavy armaments, and
increased air support enabled him to establish a
140-mile (225-km) "Pusan Perimeter," centered
on the port of Pusan. His skill in shifting reserves
to blunt North Korean attacks on the perimeter
held the line and gained time for the organization
of the X Corps under Edward M. Almond and its
landing at Inch'ŏn on September 15. The pressure
thus relieved, Walker was able to go on the offensive and push north. The Eighth Army made contact with the X Corps on September 26, and, with
some reluctance on Walker's part but on the orders
of MacArthur, they pushed together into North
Korean territory.

The ROKA I Corps took Wŏnsan, and the
U.S. I Corps took the North's capital, P'yŏngyang.
Then on November 25 a massive offensive by
Chinese forces on UN lines at the Ch'ŏngch'ŏn
River quickly turned the tide. Falling back under
extreme pressure, Walker abandoned P'yŏngyang
on December 5 and 10 days later established a
new line roughly on the 38th parallel, the original

dividing line between North and South Korea. He was killed in a jeep accident on the road between Seoul and the new front. Walker was succeeded as commander of the Eighth Army by Matthew B. Ridgway.

JAMES ALWARD VAN FLEET
(1892–1992)

James Alward Van Fleet was a U.S. military officer who was a division and corps commander during crucial World War II battles, notably the Normandy Invasion and the Battle of the Bulge, and was commander of U.S. ground forces during much of the Korean War.

Van Fleet graduated from the United States Military Academy at West Point, New York (1915), and was commissioned in the infantry. As a major during World War I, he was in charge of a machine-gun battalion and saw action at the Meuse-Argonne offensive. He spent most of the interwar years as a training instructor in Kansas,

James Van Fleet (*right*) sits with South Korean leader Syngman Rhee during a visit to a ROKA training camp.

South Dakota, Florida, and California before taking
command of the 8th Infantry Regiment in 1941. On
June 6, 1944, D-Day of the Normandy Invasion, the
8th went ashore on Utah Beach, and by June 28 it had
liberated the port city of Cherbourg. In October Van
Fleet, promoted to major general, was given command
of the 90th Division, which took part in the Ardennes
counteroffensive (Battle of the Bulge) in January 1945.
He was then given the III Corps, which in March broke
out of the Remagen bridgehead and fought through
Germany to Austria.

After his distinguished World War II service, Van
Fleet worked as deputy chief of staff of the army's
European Command in Frankfurt, West Germany. In
1948 President Harry S. Truman appointed him to
direct the military advisory missions to Greece and
Turkey, where he played a vital role in the defeat of
communist guerrillas.

In April 1951 Van Fleet was named to succeed
Matthew B. Ridgway as commander of the Eighth
Army in Korea, which included all U.S. ground
forces as well as South Korean and other units.
His command lasted through months of bitter
fighting for small tactical advantages while armistice
negotiations dragged on. He was promoted to
general in July 1951, but he grew impatient with
what he viewed as restrictions placed on his army's
ability to fight and was replaced by Maxwell Taylor
in February 1953. At that point he retired. He was
the recipient of the Purple Heart, the Distinguished
Service Cross, the Silver Star, the Bronze Star,

and, his most-prized commendation, the Combat Infantryman's Badge.

EDWARD ALMOND
(1892–1979)

Edward Almond graduated from Virginia Military Institute (VMI) in 1915 and in November 1916 took a commission in the infantry. He was promoted to captain in July 1917 and, upon the entry of the United States into World War I, served with the 4th Division in France, where he commanded a machine-gun battalion in the Aisne-Marne and Meuse-Argonne offensives. After the war he taught at a military institute in Alabama, and from 1923 to 1928 he attended and then taught at the Infantry School at Fort Benning, Georgia. Over the following years he attended the Command and General Staff School at Fort Leavenworth, Kansas, took a tour of duty in the Philippines, attended the Army War College at Carlisle Barracks, Pennsylvania, completed the course at the Naval War College at Newport, Rhode Island, and was assigned various staff duties.

Almond was promoted to temporary ranks of colonel in October 1941 and brigadier general in March 1942, soon after the United States entered World War II. In July 1942 he took command of the 92nd Division, which he trained in Alabama and Arizona until August 1944, when he took it overseas for service in Italy. The 92nd was the last all-black division in the segregated U.S. Army and the only black division to go into action as a complete unit in World War II. Its reputation in combat was tarnished by reports of low morale, incompetence, and cowardice in some units, and historians have differed ever since over the veracity of those reports and over Almond's role in the division's performance. Some have insisted that he was a fair though exacting commander of a division that suffered from neglect by the army; others have argued that he was a Southern white racist who expected little of black troops and got little in return. During the war Almond's only son and only son-in-law were killed in action in Europe.

Almond returned to the United States in August 1945. In June 1946 he was transferred to Gen. Douglas MacArthur's Far East Command head-quarters in Tokyo, eventually becoming chief of staff (with a permanent rank of major general). With the outbreak of the Korean War in June 1950, he assisted MacArthur in planning for an amphibious assault midway up the west coast of the Korean peninsula. In recognition of Almond's services, MacArthur appointed him commander of the newly created X Corps, which was assembled from two skeleton divisions and assorted other elements to execute the plan. After landing at Inch'ŏn on September 15, Almond's corps quickly took Seoul, the South Korean capital, and linked up with Gen. Walton H. Walker's Eighth Army, trapping some 120,000 North Korean troops between them. In October the X Corps moved by sea around the peninsula and landed unopposed at Wŏnsan, on the east coast of North Korea. Following MacArthur's plan, Almond pushed north and reached the Chinese border at the Yalu River by November 21, but massive Chinese counterattacks forced UN forces to withdraw. By December 11 the X Corps had concentrated in the port of Hŭngnam, whence it embarked for Pusan, South Korea—a huge operation involving 105,000 troops, nearly as many refugees, and all matériel. Incorporated into the Eighth Army, the X Corps reentered the line in east-central Korea and participated in the gradual advance back across the 38th parallel.

Almond remained in command of the X Corps until July 1951. He was then given command of the Army War College, a post he held until his retirement from the military in January 1953. In civilian life he was an executive in an insurance company and a member of the supervisory board of VMI.

MATTHEW RIDGWAY
(1895–1993)

U.S. Army general Matthew Bunker Ridgway was one of the most important U.S. military figures of the 20th century. He is known for innovative strategies developed during World War II and the Korean War.

Ridgway was born on March 3, 1895, in Fort Monroe (Hampton), Virginia. A 1917 graduate of the United States Military Academy at West Point, New York, Ridgway was assigned as an instructor at the academy during World War I. He later saw service in

China, Nicaragua, and the Philippines.

At the outbreak of World War II, Ridgway was working in the war plans division of the War Department. He was prominent in airborne services during World War II, converting the 82nd Infantry Division into the 82nd Airborne Division in 1942. Ridgway planned and led the 82nd Airborne's attack on Sicily, Italy, in 1943 and its parachute drop into Normandy, France, on D-Day in 1944.

Ridgway commanded the U.S. 8th Army in the Korean War. He rallied United Nations forces in Korea from the brink of defeat in December 1950–April 1951, when he replaced Gen. Douglas MacArthur in all commands, including the Allied

General Matthew Ridgway (*right*) reviews the Eighth Army Honor Guard with General Mark Clark. Ridgway succeeded Douglas MacArthur as UN commander in the Far East, and Clark succeeded Ridgway after he stepped down in 1952.

occupation of Japan and United Nations operations in Korea. He initiated a counteroffensive that drove the Chinese out of South Korea. Ridgway became a four-star general in May 1951. He served as commander of the North Atlantic Treaty Organization (NATO) in 1952–53 and as U.S. Army chief of staff in 1953–55. He retired in 1955. He was the author of the memoirs *Soldier* and *The Korean War*. Ridgway died on July 26, 1993, in Fox Chapel, near Pittsburgh, Pennsylvania.

MARK CLARK
(1896–1984)

A U.S. Army general during World War II, Mark Clark commanded the Allied forces during the successful Italian campaign of 1943–44. In 1945, at the age of 48, he became the youngest American to be promoted to full general.

Mark Wayne Clark was born on May 1, 1896, in Madison Barracks, New York. He graduated from the United States Military Academy in West Point, New York, in 1917 and served overseas in World War I. Early in 1942, during World War II, he became chief of staff of Army ground forces. Later that year, as deputy commander in chief to General Dwight D. Eisenhower, he executed delicate and demanding assignments in connection with the Allied invasion of North Africa.

By the end of 1942 Clark was appointed commander of the 5th Army, which landed at Salerno,

Italy, in September l943. After a hard-fought campaign, Rome was liberated in June 1944. In December of that year Clark was appointed commander of the 15th Army Group. The German forces in the north of Italy finally surrendered on May 2, 1945.

After the war Clark took command of U.S. troops in Austria before returning home to lead the 6th Army and later the army field forces. In 1952, during the Korean War, Clark was given command of all United Nations troops in Korea. He held that post until an armistice was signed in July 1953. Later that year he retired from the U.S. Army. From 1954 to 1966 he served as president of The Citadel, a military college in Charleston, South Carolina. He died in Charleston on April 17, 1984.

PENG DEHUAI
(1898–1974)

Peng Dehuai was one of the greatest military leaders in Chinese Communist history, and minister of national defense of China from 1954 until 1959, when he was removed for criticizing the military and economic policies of the party.

Peng was a military commander under a local warlord and later under Chiang Kai-shek (Jiang Jieshi) but broke with him in 1927 when Chiang attempted to rid the Nationalist Party (Kuomintang) of leftist elements. In 1928 Peng became a Communist and soon afterward became

Peng Dehuai (*left*) stands with Mao Zedong, shortly after returning from serving in the Korean War. Despite his successes during the war, he would later fall out of favor with the Mao regime.

involved in guerrilla activity, leading a series of peasant uprisings. He became a senior military commander under Mao Zedong and participated in the Long March (1934–35).

Peng was the second-ranking man in the Communists' military hierarchy from the outbreak of the Sino-Japanese War in 1937 to 1954 and was a member of the Political Bureau (Politburo) of the Chinese Communist Party (CCP) from 1936. He led Chinese forces in the Korean War and signed the armistice at P'anmunjŏm on July 27, 1953. In 1954 he became minister of national defense. In 1959, however, he criticized as impractical the policies of the Great Leap Forward, which emphasized ideological purity over professional expertise in both the military forces and the economy. Peng was deprived of office for a while and in 1965 was sent to the CCP's Southwest Bureau in Sichuan province. Peng was posthumously "rehabilitated" in December 1978 under the post-Mao regime.

PARK CHUNG HEE
(1917–79)

The president of South Korea from 1963 until 1979, Park Chung Hee left a legacy of economic development achieved in part through the severe restriction of political freedom.

Park Chung Hee was born on September 30 or November 14, 1917, to a poor, rural family near Taegu. After graduating from Taegu Normal School, Park taught primary school before entering a Japanese military academy. He served in the Japanese army during World War II. When Korea was liberated from Japanese rule, Park returned to serve in the Korean military. After the Korean War he was promoted to general.

In 1961 Park led a bloodless coup that overthrew the civilian government. He resigned as head of the ruling junta two years later and was elected president. He attracted foreign investments and transformed South Korea into an industrial nation. In the name of fighting Communism, he suppressed opposition parties and controlled the judicial system, the press, and the universities. Riots erupted when Park established diplomatic relations with Japan in 1964.

Reelected in 1967, Park introduced a constitutional amendment allowing him to serve a third term, beginning in 1971. Park declared martial law on October 17, 1972. Protests took place in 1979 when Park dismissed an opposition leader from the National Assembly. Following two previous assassination attempts, Park was killed by the head of the Korean Central Intelligence Agency on October 26, 1979, in Seoul.

CHUNG IL KWON
(1917–94)

Chung Il Kwon was a Korean army officer and politician and the commander of South Korean troops during some of the most intense fighting against North Korean and Chinese forces during the Korean War.

Chung was a 1940 graduate of Tokyo's Military Academy and served in Japan's Imperial Army in Manchuria during World War II. He then joined the Chinese Nationalist army before entering the Republic of Korea Army (ROKA). After North Korean troops invaded South Korea in June 1950, Chung was made commander of all ROKA forces. He led ROKA units during the difficult retreat in July–August to Pusan, in coordination with the U.S. Eighth Army, and also during the surprise landing in September at Inch'ŏn, which crippled the North Korean offensive.

Chung Il Kwon (*left*) meets with Dwight Eisenhower (*second from left*) and other U.S. military leaders during the Korean War. The ROKA forces under Chung saw many successes and were instrumental during the Pusan retreat and the Inch'on landing.

Hailed as a national hero, Chung was made chairman of the South Korean joint chiefs of staff in 1956, and he retired from the military in 1957 as a four-star general. During his retirement he was ambassador to the United States, France, and several Latin American countries. He also served as prime minister (1964–70) under Pres. Park Chung Hee, a fellow former military officer who had seized power in 1961. Chung then held a number of government posts before Chun Doo Hwan assumed the presidency in 1980.

CONCLUSION

In the years following the Korean War, South Korea continued to enjoy a strong relationship with the West. North Korea, however, consistently showed belligerence to the South and its Western allies. Even after the collapse of the Soviet Union, the Korean peninsula would continue to be caught in the coils of Cold War rivalry. In 2013 North Korea once again began a dramatic escalation of its rhetoric against the United States and South Korea, including verbal threats of missile attacks against both countries. It also cut off all lines of emergency communication with the government in Seoul, barred South Korean workers from entering the joint industrial zone in Kaesŏng, and declared the Korean War armistice void.

Leaving a still-divided Korea and resulting in over one million total combat casualties, little about the Korean War could or should be forgotten. On a global level, it pitted the United States against the world's major Communist powers and represented one of the most significant military conflicts of the Cold War. It also marked the first limited war fought in the age of nuclear power. On the individual scale, the Korean War saw the rise of numerous political and military heavyweights, whose historic contributions are still felt in foreign policy today. Despite the war's ending in stalemate and the turbulent politics of the North, the survival and flourishing of South Korea has kept alive the hope of civil liberties, democracy, economic development, and eventual unification—even if their fulfillment might require another 50 years or more.

GLOSSARY

amphibious Executed by coordinated action of land, sea, and air forces organized for invasion.

armistice An agreement to stop fighting a war.

artillery Large guns that are used to shoot over a great distance.

attrition The act or process of weakening and gradually defeating an enemy through constant attacks and continued pressure over a long period of time.

Bolshevik A member of the extremist wing of the Russian Social Democratic Party, which seized power in Russia by the Revolution of November 1917.

Cold War The open yet restricted rivalry and hostility that developed after World War II between the United States and the Soviet Union and their respective allies and that ended with the collapse of the Soviet Union in 1991.

commissar The head of a government department in the Union of Soviet Socialist Republics until 1946.

Communism The political and economic doctrine that aims to replace private property and a profit-based economy with public ownership and communal control of at least the major means of production (e.g., mines, mills, and factories) and the natural resources of a society.

constabulary The police force of a particular area.

containment Strategic U.S. foreign policy of the late 1940s and early 1950s intended to check the expansionist designs of the Soviet Union through economic, military, diplomatic, and political means.

guerrilla A member of a usually small group of soldiers who do not belong to a regular army and who fight in a war as an independent unit; of or relating to such individuals.

infantry A branch of an army made up of soldiers trained, armed, and equipped to fight on foot.

limited war A war whose objective is less than the total defeat of the enemy.

Marxist Of or related to the political, economic, and social theories of Karl Marx, including the belief that the struggle between social classes is a major force in history and that there should eventually be a society in which there are no classes.

nationalist Of or relating to a political group that wants to form a separate and independent nation.

Politburo The principal policy-making and executive committee of a Communist Party.

propaganda Ideas or statements that are often false or exaggerated and that are spread in order to help a cause, a political leader, a government, etc.

repatriate To restore or return to the country of origin, allegiance, or citizenship.

retrograde Returning to an earlier and usually worse state or condition.

stalemate A contest, dispute, war, etc., in which neither side can gain an advantage or win.

The Army Historical Foundation

2425 Wilson Boulevard

Arlington, VA 22201

(800) 506-2672

Website: https://armyhistory.org

The Army Historical Foundation is a nonprofit
organization dedicated to preserving the
stories and artifacts of the U.S. Army, restoring
important historical buildings and landmarks
related to the Army, and supporting the
National Museum of the United States Army.

Canadian War Museum

1 Vimy Place

Ottawa, ON K1A 0M8

Canada

(800) 555-5621

Website: http://www.warmuseum.ca

Through exhibitions featuring art, artifacts, and
memoirs, as well as interactive presentations,
the Canadian War Museum engages visitors
with the history of the Canadian military from
its inception to the present. It also offers a
variety of educational programs on the history
of the Canadian armed forces.

The Korean War National Museum (KWNM)

Denis J. Healy Freedom Center

9 S. Old State Capitol Plaza

Springfield, IL 62701

(888) 419-5053

Website: http://kwnm.org

The KWNM honors the legacy of the Korean War and its veterans through its exhibits and artifacts. Visitors will learn about the history of the war and its aftermath as well as incredible acts of heroism and sacrifice.

Korean War Veterans Association (KWVA)

P.O. Box 407

Charleston, IL 61920

(217) 345-4414

Website: http://www.kwva.org

The KWVA supports veterans who served in Korea as part of the U.S. Armed Forces as well as their families and establishes and maintains memorials around the United States. It also distributes *The Graybeards*, the official publication of the organization.

Korean War Veterans Memorial

900 Ohio Drive SW

Washington, DC 20024

(202) 426-6841

Website: http://www.nps.gov/kowa/index.htm

Located on the National Mall in Washington, D.C., the Korean War Veterans Memorial honors the service of the 5.8 million Americans who served in the Korean War.

National Museum of the Marine Corps

18900 Jefferson Davis Highway

Triangle, VA 22172

(877) 635-1775

Website: http://www.usmcmuseum.com/index.asp

The National Museum of the Marine Corps collects and preserves the material history of the United States Marine Corps through exhibits and research. Its Korean War Gallery introduces visitors to the politics of the conflict and describes the Marines' vital role in key battles and events.

National Museum of the U.S. Navy

805 Kidder Breese Street SE

Washington Navy Yard, DC 20374

(202) 433-4882

Website: http://www.history.navy.mil/museums/ NationalMuseum/org8-1.htm

The National Museum of the U.S. Navy hosts a collection of some of the most important naval artifacts in the history of the United States Navy. Its numerous exhibits include *Korea 1950–53: The Navy in the Forgotten War.* It also hosts an on-site library, archives, and photographic and other research facilities.

Naval Historical Foundation (NHF)

1306 Dahlgren Avenue Southeast

Washington Navy Yard, DC 20374

(888) 880-0102

Website: http://www.navyhistory.org

The NHF works to promote and teach the history of the United States Navy, hosting large archives of important naval manuscripts and other historical documents, as well as an on-site museum with exhibits on naval history.

Royal Canadian Regiment Museum

701 Oxford Street East

London, ON N5Y 4T7

Canada

(519) 660-5275 ext. 5015

Website: http://thercr.ca/main/index.php/ the-rcr-museum-new

The Royal Canadian Regiment Museum chronicles Royal Canadian Regiment's history of service since 1883. Exhibits, including one on the Korean War, showcase weapons and equipment used by the regiment in various conflicts as well as medals awarded to the soldiers.

WEBSITES

Because of the changing nature of Internet links, Rosen Publishing has developed an online list of websites related to the subject of this book. This site is updated regularly. Please use this link to access this list:

http://www.rosenlinks.com/WAR/Korea

Alexander, Bevin. *MacArthur's War: The Flawed Genius Who Challenged the American Political System*. New York, NY: Berkley Books, 2013.

Cumings, Bruce. *The Korean War*. New York, NY: Modern Library, 2011.

Halberstam, David. *The Coldest Winter*. New York, NY: Hyperion, 2007.

Hammes, T.X. *Forgotten Warriors: The 1st Provisional Marine Brigade, the Corps Ethos, and the Korean War*. Lawrence, KS: The University Press of Kansas, 2010.

Haruki, Wada. *The Korean War: An International History*. Lanham, MD: Rowman and Littlefield, 2014.

Immell, Myra. *The Korean War*. San Diego, CA: Greenhaven, 2011.

Malkasian, Carter. *The Korean War*. New York, NY: Rosen Publishing, 2009.

Millett, Allan R. *The War for Korea, 1950–1951: They Came From the North*. Lawrence, KS: University Press of Kansas, 2010.

Moore, Shannon Baker. *Korean War*. Minneapolis, MN: ABDO, 2014.

Mulholland, Andrew. *The Korean War: History in an Hour*. London, UK: William Collins, 2013.

Perry, Mark. *The Most Dangerous Man in America: The Making of Douglas MacArthur*. New York, NY: Basic Books, 2014.

Richardson, Bill, and Kevin Maurer. *Valleys of Death: A Memoir of the Korean War*. New York, NY: Berkley, 2010.

Senker, Cath. *North Korea and South Korea*. New York, NY: Rosen Publishing, 2013.

Sloan, Bill. *The Darkest Summer: Pusan and Inchon 1950: The Battles That Saved South Korea—and the Marines—From Extinction*. New York, NY: Simon and Schuster, 2010.

Weintraub, Stanley. *A Christmas Far From Home: An Epic Tale of Courage and Survival During the Korean War*. Boston, MA: Da Capo Press, 2014.

Yu, Yŏng-ik. *The Making of the First Korean President: Syngman Rhee's Quest for Independence*. Honolulu, HI: University of Hawaii Press, 2014.